THE ART OF DYING

THE HUGH MACLENNAN POETRY SERIES

Editors: Allan Hepburn and Carolyn Smart

The Art of Dying

Sarah Tolmie

McGill-Queen's University Press
Montreal & Kingston • London • Chicago

ISBN 978-0-7735-5271-5 (paper)
ISBN 978-0-7735-5272-2 (ePDF)
ISBN 978-0-7735-5273-9 (ePUB)

Legal deposit first quarter 2018
Bibliothèque nationale du Québec

Printed in Canada on acid-free paper that is 100% ancient forest free (100% post-consumer recycled), processed chlorine free

McGill-Queen's University Press acknowledges the support of the Canada Council for the Arts for our publishing program. We also acknowledge the financial support of the Government of Canada through the Canada Book Fund for our publishing activities.

Library and Archives Canada Cataloguing in Publication

Tolmie, Sarah, 1971–, author
    The art of dying / Sarah Tolmie.

    (The Hugh MacLennan poetry series)
    Poems.
    Issued in print and electronic formats.
    ISBN 978-0-7735-5271-5 (softcover).–
    ISBN 978-0-7735-5272-2 (ePDF).–
    ISBN 978-0-7735-5273-9 (ePUB)

    I. Title. II. Series: Hugh MacLennan poetry series

    PS8639.O45A78 2018   C811'.6   C2017-904235-1
                                             C2017-904236-X

This book was typeset by Marquis Interscript
in 9.5/13 New Baskerville.

THE ART OF DYING

Hate to tell you, but you're going to die.
Quite soon. Me, too.

Shuck off the wisdom while it's warm.
Death does no harm
To wisdom.

Poets no longer rate so high
In the consolation industry.
We have been fools.

TV has usurped our role:
Zombies, vampires, doctors, priests
Tell us our deaths need not be.

Our friends spam us from the internet
With the final selfie that death photobombed.
Truth is becalmed.

The scholastics had a category they
Used to measure ubiquity:
Things like water, or air; things that were not scarce.

Their value lay in the cost of their possible loss.
Human life is ubiquitous.
But of course it means quite a lot to us.

Cancer survivors use a different math.
They count out from a death survived and passed,
Marking new birthdays: one year cancer-free, then two
And five and ten. It makes them young again.

They've let go the notion that they're owed
That set amount of life we all subtract from as we go –
Threescore years and ten or so.

Go on, you know you do.
Unfair, we say, unfair unfair
Like some referee is standing there.

Our sorrow is an estimate:
Where is my entitlement?
The minutes on my plan?
Return for all I've paid in rent?

Angels, demons, elves, AI
Don't die, and live in elegy,
Preaching in books and on TV
About the sterile banality of their immortality.

What else would you expect of elves?
We know we'd do just fine ourselves.

Though Wittgenstein, wise man, did say
Eternal life would not make mystery go away.

6

The dead light fires inside our squelching brains,
Small beacons cast from path to path
Across the damp synapses of our memory lanes.

There they encamp and warm their tiny hands
And frailly live again.
How can we preserve their tiny flames?

Could it be that you'll remember lines
Of dialogue, or song lyrics instead
Of your mother's or your brother's face?

That they will come to stand in for the dead?
Unless you remember some exact few things they said?
Words. They stick in your head.

Old photos, hermetically sealed,
Dreary haircuts, weary smiles,
On Throwback Thursday's faded child:
Their captions are gargantuan.

Tiny poems, single words
Above the frame, those sketch the person in.

There oughtta be a law
Against the phrase "pass on."
Or even, "pass." You heard that one?

"She passed." Well done!
Flunk out of life; death still takes you on.

Euphemism is the cheapest metaphor
In the aisle of the dollar store
Along with the headless Barbies and obscure bits of bright
plastic.

It continues fashionable to mourn the death of ritual.
We miss the Neolithic ochre, smoking censers, silly hats
Cthulhu and Harryhausen prayers, all the mystic flap.

No one has ever owned death much better than that.
Still, ours are not that bad.
Hospitals have strict norms,

Specific times and tricky forms,
Rotting fruit and flowers.
We say conventional things at canonical hours.

Or, you can have a conscious hippie death
In your own bed with body paint and different drugs,
Mandalas, power circles, sweet grass, hugs
And a green coffin that converts
You straight to mushrooms in the yard.

Death still gets the final word.

We used to teach our children gruesome prayers
To alleviate their nightly fears.
Now I lay me down to sleep –

How sick is that?
I guess they functioned to distract
From the main mystery.

What on earth's a God?
A huge beneficent force that claims a soul that I can't find?
How is that supposed to relieve my mind?

Oh God, he saves me when I'm dead
And my body just lies on here in my bed?

Death's hard enough to fathom in your face.
It causes eight-year-old hearts to race at night
As they contemplate the idea.

They come and wake you and they grip your hands
And you cuddle them and say you understand, it's all okay,
They are not going to die *today*.

Death is supposed to be like sleep.
Well, not for me.
Sleep's quite lively.

These days, I dream so vividly I wake exhausted.
In sleep I come, and learn, and sweat, and fear,
No danger of not being here.

Before, it was an endless chase down corridors,
Evasive bull, flagging toreador,
Flapping my banner ragged.

My daughter wakes up mummified,
Wrapped in her blankets every time
From nightly flailing.

My son is found bum upward,
Wrapped around a three-foot-long stuffed frog,
Or thrown drastically down the bed's end, dropped from a
    plane.

Sleep extends the squirms of day.
We do not sleep cadaverously.

Cats have nine lives.
Gamers have many more,
Lives and lives, each one a prize.

More life, more health, more points, more wealth,
More trades, more guns, more shots, more tools,
Arsenals and seven-league boots.

I've heard my children say, in pure ennui,
Kill me now to get me past this screen.
Death is a passing strategy.

The only embalmer I know personally
Is fond of the Dead Kennedys.
He plays atrocious punk while very decorously
Cutting out people's guts.
He does painstaking, earnest work of high technique:

The final, inverse surgery.
Thrash and grunge and acid rock
Death metal and electro-pop
Leak out of his prep rooms non-stop
Until they're drowned out by the Bach in the lobby.

Ars moriendi once was written by the pound
And *danse macabre* graced church walls in every town.
Europe is kinky, no?

Advice on how to die – just who needs that?
Here's *How to Be a Tasteless Prat, How to Be Obnoxious, Rude
     and Fat,*
How to Be Constantly Terrified, bestsellers all.

And yet, in fearful gallantry,
The skeletons
Danced awesomely.

Plants have their own zen.
They live their lives at different speeds.
They're horny things,

Breeding, blooming, casting seeds abroad,
Determined to succeed.
And we perceive their slow urgency

Pleasurably.
Except those who suffer from allergies
Who get tired of being raped by trees.

Some plants are perennial.
These we leave from year to year.
About annuals we are more casual,

Ripping them up at season's end
Compunctionless.
Only through their beauty they defend

Their places in our gardens,
First to fall prey to every change in plan.
Ours is no better mercy than the wind's.

I stepped on a snail today.
The poor thing popped gently, like a Rice Krispie.
Didn't even bruise my heel.
Still, I did feel like an idiot, having carefully
Plucked it from a tomato leaf and set it out of harm's way.

In some, the thought of death produces panic.
Some get depressed and some get manic; some
Repress all thoughts of it entirely.

Conservatives, we've heard, have death anxiety.
Pundits say they're from a retro world
Where quick response to threat keeps you alive:

That primal scene, the Pleistocene.
Hierarchy, order, form, these keep them calm
And fast recoil helps them to live long.

Liberals do better with contingency,
Although nothing ever seems
To make them happy.

It's a relief to realize
That death, at least, is standardized.

Death makes for monuments.
Ponderous cenotaphs, to be sure,
But it combats the miniature.

The purview of poets has become so small:
The whorls on every snail's shell,
Pure form and sound, or ranting farce,

We've painted ourselves right out of art.

Most books of poems are far too short.
It's hard to get your money's worth.
How does it make sense in the marketplace

To pay twelve quid for sixty pages?
Or fifteen euros, or twenty bucks?
So poets are shit out of luck.

Stuck in the dinky bijou suite
As the ship sinks titanically.
Editors sob to publishing houses

While the novel-reading mob is out carousing.
We're supposed to be commensurate to the greats,
While students sink beneath the burgeoning weight

Of the Norton anthology?
Those who read, they buy whole series –
Thousands of pages, millions of words,

While we keep polishing the same few turds,
Constipated. Holy crap.
Time for this business to lighten up.

I wish she just wrote books instead,
Said my philistine friend, about Alice Munro.
Collections are boring, you know?

All the same. I want some flow.
After my heartbeat had slowed,
I thought, maybe she has a point.

There's no shortage of disjointedness.
When's the last time you missed your stop
Reading a series of disparate thoughts?

Poets should be allowed to write books, too.
Have an idea and see it through,
With a bit of a plot or a big fat theme

That makes it okay for readers to read.
Just read. Not be put on the spot
To have a big think every twenty lines.

Thinking is really just fine.
But I'm not a Fitbit made for your mind,
Here to whittle your taste down a couple of sizes.

I was drinking with a code jockey the other day
And he put down his glass and said plaintively,
You know what's wrong with poetry?
I said hey boy, why don't you tell me?

He didn't even rise. Just looked at me and sighed.
You know what would be punk rock?
If a poet ended a line and stopped
With a rhyme. Or not. With a rhyme. Or not

With a rhyme just part of the time. Then we'd know
Where we are. Things would be more clear.
He looked at me and I looked severe.
I said, son, if you start in with zero and one

I will break your face. Okay?
I'm really done with that analogy.
Fine, he said, and sat there, glum.
I agree, I said, but it's mine to say.

So he finished his beer and he went away.

Poets, like rabbits, have short attention spans.
Frozen or twitchy, noses and hands.
While slow and steady wins the race
We're the ones running in place.

Badger novelists undermine our thumping feet
And down we go, and then they eat
Us.

Novelists read poets. They're the precious few,
Except for poets, and who cares what they do?
Then they regurgitate at length, with characters,
Books with a story that you read straight through,

The fuckers. So we're doomed
To be the *entr'acte*, the precious tasting menu.
Lyric is a wank.
Novelists and their agents howl to the bank.

Sad memoirists follow in their wake,
Forgetting that a life worth spit will already speak.
You live or write. You are Watson or Holmes.
Very few of us can safely play both roles.

Poetry is dead, of that I'm sure,
And yet I fuss about my angle in the snare.

There's no shortage of books that teach us how to live.
Every quarter multiplies imperatives:
How to be rich, thin, resilient, eco, cool;
How to pick up women, do your makeup, cheat in school.

Of these skills, we poets impart few.
We've kind of lost the common ground.
This is our moment to dig down.

The ground is where we're headed, every one:
Picked clean by endangered vultures, burnt and sprinkled
    round,
Tucked tight in urns or boxed neat underground.

Death's the one place that finally evades
All news, all ties, all gender, race and creed.
Where we dissolves to I and dissipates, relieved.

The world is old.
We dig up bones, not helms or gold.
History is extinct.

Our kids name stars and dinosaurs
And have never heard of Rome.
Their stories start so long ago.

The only diaspora they know is the Big Bang.
Atoms collide and lava flows beneath tectonic plates.
Units must be minuscule or huge to register.

Tribes and empires that come and go
At human scale – decades or centuries, a millennium or two –
Just do not show.

How horrified the Babylonians would be
To face this double jeopardy.

Fortunately, they'll never know.

Many kids fantasize about blowing up their schools.
I should have pressed the button on one or two.
This year, my kids will get to watch theirs die.

The old school will be primed, and blown, and smashed,
Each room in which their tiny asses sat on tiny chairs
Exploded, the grass out back built over.

Feelings will be mixed. I expect some solemn poems.
Bricks will be collected and buried in due form.
Elegy's addictive. They will have all year.

Good days they will weep; bad days they will cheer.
People stand on darkened thresholds, staring at the ground.
Then they run out back and kick a ball around.

Hedonism is widely blamed on death.
We forget pleasure and its genuine appeal.
I see these people gathered here
Eating ribs and drinking beer,

Listening to the blues
And talking to their friends.
I doubt they're waiting for the world to end.

You and I will die of STDs
Or hardening of the arteries,
Not in grand defiance of our fate
But in quest of something nice to do today.

Remember Robert Mapplethorpe and how
He could make a flower
Look like a throat laid open with a straight razor?

Or those guys, all bronzed and suave, whose dicks
He wanted to cut off and arrange, three to a vase,
But could not, as there are laws?

Still life. He brought it to a head.
Most things are still when they are dead.
Stupendous piles of fruit, dewed grapes, split

Oysters, velvet drapes and skulls.
The beauty of bourgeois accoutrement, shiny and neat;
Soutine's sonatines to hanging meat.

The same, he said.

I had to abort a fetus once at fourteen weeks.
That sucked but was less agony
Than its putative life, all back to front, a wreck.

Such moments of naked horror let us see
The bloodyminded fervour of the selfish gene.
If you look around you, you will learn

Almost every woman that you know
Has lost a baby or two.
Lost. As if you left it on the bus

Or it just fell out of your uterus
In a Monty Python sketch.
Behind the screen of this careful word,

The old truths of the sisterhood:
Not to be judged, or feared, or harmed
Because of a child not in your arms.

We're all aware that human hair is dead
Yet we spend thousands taking care of it.
It's like an endless funeral.

The moment your hair hits air, it's toast.
It only lives inside the follicle.
That we twist and burn and fry it,

Straighten it and dye it, does not surprise.
What's it gonna do, spit out your cheap shampoo?
We worry about its body and its strength: an athlete.

We buy nourishing products. It doesn't eat.
One hundred thousand lovers, infants, metaphors
Of keratin, our stone dead hairs.

Ancient Egyptians were well groomed in death.
My daughter's reading about them now
To improve her French grammar.

Morbid topics are okay
In the name of vocabulary.
Who knows what you might have to say

In France, today? Excuse me, could you assist
In pulling my brain out through my nose?
There's an exquisite tool.

Here. Yes. Thanks. Is that your slave?
No? I only thought he looked like one.
It's hard to get them to behave.

Fresh out of myrrh? That is a shame.
We can use argan oil instead.
It is fair trade.

And so on. I'm at the spa today, you see,
Such musings naturally arise
Where we are poached in steam

And our follicles are fried;
Where we are draped on racks
And pummelled, towelled, dried;

Where our flesh is preserved.
I went into the bathroom and observed
In the corner a perfect canister

Wrapped in faux leather, with a neat lid,
Wherein three rolls of toilet paper hid
So decorously that it was clear

They were part of a ceremony
Of waste elimination. I looked round for the priest.
I paid the bill and realized it was me.

Metaphors also die. They fossilize,
Becoming pigs in pokes or dying on the vine.
Language is full of sedimentary layers

Containing spiky phrases that were once alive.
These can be memorized and still function just fine
But they're not much fun. Lose the manual and you're done.

The juicy ones you make up on the fly.
They're fully naturalized. A is like B.
A's B. That's all it takes. You do it all the time.

Congratulations! You're a poet, too.
Start filling out the forms.
Poetry is thought. That's its universal charm.

You itch to smoke. Your boss, is she
Truly a bitch? You see? The list goes on.

Parasites eat raw food.
We're still alive, right?
Nice and fresh.

Some people think our food's too dead.
Inert. Unappetizing. Nutrient-poor.
Slaughtered, cruelly uprooted, shipped too far.

We buy tomatoes on the vine,
Lettuces and herbs still packed in dirt
In an effort to repent.

Juice bars boom selling the blood of fruit,
New squeezed.
A place that just sells sprouts

Is opening quite near our house.
If we eat their lives, and not their deaths
We'll never die, I guess.

Why can't I hire a death coach?
Surely death is still in growth.

Murderers practice what they preach,
Though their instructions may be brief.

Men in armies must discuss how fatal wounds
Are not just given but received.

Torturers may use the word and do the deed
Though it is not death, but pain, that is their specialty.

Hospice workers, nurses in palliative care,
Practically help us to prepare.

Churches insist it's not death, anyway.
Perhaps this is my opportunity.

Many dead things address us.
The worst are bank machines.
I hate it when they use my name.

You work half your life to have a job in which you don't
Have it stitched on your lapel
And computers use it, casual as hell.

Fuck off. Where is the fuck-off button,
If we must have this conversation?
Voices speak abroad to the insane.

I know my name. I see no need
To pretend that stream of numbers recognizes me.

Michael Jackson had a Lazarus fail.
He always did things on the grand scale,
Having himself euthanized nightly.

Finally it stuck.
The doc went out to smoke or make a call
And he never woke up.

Widespread woe, tributes, lawsuits ensued
But one thing everybody knew
Was all his wealth did him no good.

This is counterintuitive
And makes us slightly, cruelly pleased
At the death of celebrities.

Salve frater atque vale.

Robin Williams died today, a suicide.
The internet's aflame with chat.
He was depressed. It's no surprise.

He killed himself. Let's not mince words.
Depressives get it.
But then, we're disturbed.

Oliver Sacks is going to die,
He tells us blithely in the *New York Times*.
He's 81. His liver's shot.

He's blind in one eye
Though when both worked fine
He could still get lost in a parking lot.

He's extremely famous and terribly shy.
He's lost his leg but it's still attached.
He's been practicing dying, Oliver Sacks.

He will do it well,
Politely evading heaven and hell.
Doctor Oliver Sacks, farewell.

The mayor whom everybody hates
(Except, apparently, the majority)
Just dropped out of the municipal race.

Cancer of the gut. And, guess what?
No one will admit how much they wished for it.
Vicious commentators feign

Polite regret, condolences are sent.
Suddenly we're sitting on the fence
Holding thought's smoking gun.

Do you want him dead, or mayor?
Those are your options, dear taxpayer.
And now you've never thought of it before?

You didn't kill him with your mind.
It was not assassination or divine
Justice. Chance, genes and fat. He dies,

And leaves the office clear. Don't tell me you're upset.
It's just your superstitious fear of Death.
Endorse his choice, and tactlessly agree,

He'll get you next time. You, and you, and me.
So what? The mayor was still a swine.
Due process failed. Let's hear it for the scythe.

Could you write a book about poetry and death
Without one mention of Sylvia Plath?
Well, I tried. I got this far,

But collapsed from the weight of her avatar:
The poet suicide of modern times.
We all know her because she died.

It was a masterstroke.
Ted Hughes is shunned
As miles of dark liner run

In contemplation of her antidote:
She who makes the system out a liar.
A good death, in a woman, we admire.

Death looks a lot like success.
As in, "I killed that test"
"She slays me" and the rest –

Though it's the act and not the state
Whose power we appropriate,
All us murderous wannabes
In our casual hyperboles.

43

Marcus Aurelius was a cool guy
Who made a virtue of necessity.
Stoicism has its flaws for those of us not emperors, however.

Men of low birth
Rarely measure themselves against the universe
And women, never.

I would make a terrible vegetarian.
Serious cooks who are not monks cook meat.
That's why humans have this kind of teeth.

The roasts of grandmothers past may put us off;
I saw a lot of this in Britain.
And nostalgic people cling

Like death to religious prohibition.
Then there is health,
The wealth that western people hoard.

Animal welfare is long past hoping for.
Animals live as we permit them and no more
And more have lived as food than ever have lived before:

A net gain, at least, in tasty quadrupeds.
The environment is doomed
And owned by people who aren't you.

If you said: I am afraid to die,
Afraid of saturated fat, I'd believe that.
If you said: I could not eat my cat,

So why a cow? I'd start to doubt. Why not?
A wasp is drowning in my wine right now. Who gives a shit?
A bee I'd carefully pour out and mop him down.

I loved horses as a child and I've eaten them in France.
I would eat my children after some horrible mischance.
I would eat up every scrap in an act of love,

As I would permit them also to eat me,
Though not wholly without fears of CJD.
Flesh is matter that converts to energy.

Time heals all wounds, they say.
Not true. Some kill you and some always stay.
Time will, though, take all wounders away.

Eventually. Eventually.

The old infuriate,
With their blinking turtle eyes,
Pervasive fears and worn-out lies,

Complacent and yet terrified
That somehow they have survived
Unto this day.

And you may not.
But then – you may.

Dead on. Dead right. Dead heat. Dead even.
Just can't get off that stairway to heaven.
Death makes metaphors just as well as sex.

Now they stand in inverse relation:
Fucking is frank and death a shibboleth.
To the Victorians it was different.

People died by fine degrees, in plainest sight,
At home in bed or in the street, in madhouses and
    dormitories.
Women were imagined on their knees

Wearing more clothes, by coffins. Bereavement
Was their kink. They celebrated
What we cannot think.

Sea stars barf up their stomachs to engulf their prey.
Their mouths are too small for any other way.
So much for intelligent design.

Life is brutal and malign in the sea, as Ted Hughes said.
No one is friends.
You live in hell. It might take ten days to dissolve your shell.

What can I say about political deaths?
I'm a poet, not an activist.
I couldn't beat your Twitter feed,
That chorus of Greek tragedy.

Poetry is not protest, except
To protestors and Protestants.
Death is not exceptional.
It is, in fact, the rule.

Often, in denial of our own
We invoke the privilege of concern
For those remote from us,

As though only the poor died, or the oppressed,
In some rare loss of their franchise,
While we remain, eternally, alive.

The internet's the place to get things off your chest.
For fast retorts. *Bon mots.* The universal therapist.
Hookups, snuff flicks, recipes

Lists of friends and enemies.
The place is rife.
But it isn't life.

Not by a stretch.
Nor is it death.
Only Purgatory.

Where we repeat the story
Until it comes out right.

Spam is dead, great Spam is dead –
Will be the epitaph of the internet
The day it powers down and we go back to skinning goats.

After it goes rogue and kills us all, almost
And we huddle on the ping-pong ball of the burnt world
And re-invent the printing press.

Poets and cave painters then will rule
Holding fast our simple tools.

So, you've been waiting, right,
For the title to invert:
The art of dying, the dying of art?

No dice.

Art never dies, it just annoys from time to time.

A *sunset plan.* That means they've cut your funds.
Whatever you thought you were, well, that is gone.
But you're not dead. Assistants are paid off

And desks move rooms. Accountants check the books.
Handshakes, golden or bronze, are offered.
Protests that arise are quickly baffled.

A plaque or two may change,
And in their dull glow
You see the sketchy outlines of things you might have known.

54

Sci-fi geeks care about the stars.
I don't know why.
Nothing about the sky impresses me.

Unearthly immensity just leaves me cold.
I'd rather read the book,
And that book's too big to read.

Our math scarcely works out there.
It's just stochastics, probabilities.
Errors a billion miles wide

And insane spans of pointless time.
Stellar physics is a cold romance,
As relevant as watching angels dance

On the heads of pins.
Cosmologists are our theologians.
They think beautiful thoughts, as Hubble takes the money
    shots

From far away. Space as a final refuge is a fantasy.
The sci-fi geeks look up, to the starry shore,
The two-handed engine smites, once and then no more.

Finally, as I age, I get big tits.
Hurray! I've waited long enough for this.
There they are. Boom boom. I love it.
Cleavage. Some notice my face above it, yakking away.

But these guys come with a use-by date.
(Yes, mine are guys. Okay?)
I cram them in line in their corsetry,
Thinking of mom's dual mastectomy.

Like Angelina, perhaps I should just lop them now –
Pre-emptively? But where's the fun in that?
We don't get to enjoy our fat?

Hormones, drugs, anxiety, bacon, wine,
In ascending order bring me to my time.
They bought the boobs and they may take them back.

People are better at a remove.
That's why dead guys are best.
Proximity's a cheap effect.

People are improved by death.
If improvement's what you want,
Stay out of the agora.

Pain and error everywhere
Bad politics and worse hair
Lies, disingenuousness.

This is of course why love exists.
Love, that coping mechanism
That lets you live while something isn't

Wholly satisfactory.
The dead are all that they can be.
Nothing wasted. What they have, they show.

And if they did nothing, they are gone
And once again your time's your own.

57

Death, too, has been Disneyfied.
Overseen by Peter Pan, the worms have turned and left the can
And measles spread from Disneyland.

Lives too privileged, healthy, quiet,
Look at death and just deny it.
Anti-vaxxers, toxic fools

Congregate their children in rich schools,
Stupefied by their own egos.
Like monks waiting for the plague

Behind the flimsy barricade of their vocation.
When their children could be saved, and mine,
And yours, by vaccination.

The world is run by economists.
Everywhere we look, we see the word *risk*.
It has a k, like *ski* or *kink* or *rusk*.
Most of our words with k are Norse.
The Vikings were not risk-averse.
Their letters travelled with their force.
Now they're brave enough to stay at home and concentrate
   on keeping warm,
Not going crazy, letting women rule.
The risks have changed Ultima Thule.

I just received a handy prompt
From the Canadian government
That will help me estimate the risk
Of cancer: prostate, breast, ovary, cervix,
Inherent in my life.
Thank God the paternal state
Will help me regulate my weight in terms of risk
Instead of sin.
It could be worse.

I'm not a libertarian.
I believe in social medicine.
We pay taxes and we cost the state a bomb.
Taking good advice will do no harm.
The language of risk exerts its charm.
A risk's a real thing, we think. A risk is run,
Daringly, upside-down, from a trapeze,
Not doggedly, drunk, on the small track in town.
Risk's a heroic vapour that we breathe.

And there are risks we shun. Our kids
Cross at the light. Hurried people let them by.
It's a risk to miss the meeting but a worse one if they die.
The law is dead and empathy is weak.
So risk is the language that we mutually speak,
The guardian of all. Risk spreads its harpy wings
And commands respect for persons and for things
Or blinding pain. Risk is cruel and sharp.
We're blood-eagled in its grasp. It is Norse at heart.

At least two people whom I knew
Wanted an assisted suicide.
Instead, they died at length, in fear and pain.

It is grotesque and cruel
That we can buy new boobs and dose our brains
To alleviate our suffering,

That we are born in teams with every kind of help
And can be made to stay alive beyond our ken,
But when we want to die, no one helps us then.

But now they will. Amen.
A short anthem now is due:
O Canada

Land of oil, trees, harpoons,
You got this one right.
Thank you.

60

Death does not end co-dependence.
Isn't this what culture means –
Alive and dead in solidarity?

Yet what is it that we see
When a parent dies, and one remains?
Half a person, wandering in pain.

Culture is strong. It tells us what to do.
It bridges the great spans with rules.
Still, we fall between the stools

After the funeral.

In this, precisely, is love cruel:
It does not die at death
But borrows tools from immortality.

Tools that do not fit the hand:
Drills that gouge the walls, saws too strong to bend,
Hammers with claws that rend our houses tearing out a nail.

Would it not be better to forget
Our loved ones at their deaths?
People speak of intersubjectivity

Like it's a great thing: I am you and you are me
And so on. Then what happens when
You die, and I am left

Half-massed? A drifting ship, unballasted?
The brain's one lonely hemisphere?
When you're half gone

And I'm half here.

Facebook is a morbid tool
That makes us fat, complacent, anxious, rude,
Comment-obstreperous, otherwise subdued.

Endlessly alarmed and pacified.
Now it's birthdays for those who've died.
Dear Dad (old photo attached), happy birthday, wish you
  were here,

Even though you died last year. Would've been ninety-five.
Congratulations! Another year you're not alive.
What are these for? Read out the parish rolls,

Include our friends in heaven, raked over the coals?
Truth is, the system gave a prompt,
Part of its daily info-dump of funerals,

Weddings, traffic delays, the birthdays of the dead
It keeps on file in hope that they'll still pay.
And we play along, just like the good old days.

Social media, in its Protestant haze,
Assumes that awareness in our brains

Has moral force. How so?
No one keeps track inside your skull.

4000 people die in an accident in Kathmandu.
It makes no difference whether you approve.

You don't get points for attitude.
There is no universal force

That by clicking like you will endorse.
Or that endorses you.

You may build your team
And foster a like-minded dream

But that's after the fact.
The fact's divorced.

A fact can be deployed
To make you happy or annoyed

But sharing it online is not a choice
Of any moral moment.

Long-distance outrage doesn't foment
Mass uprisings, change the laws, do the dirty work of any cause.

Thought never does, and words, far-off, quite rarely.
I may penalize social media unfairly

As a vehicle of liberal illusion
But that snark's long turned out a boojum.

There are several kinds of black death.
Septicemic, bubonic and pneumatic plague. The pest.
It has killed a lot of us,

Carried by fleas and rats and Asian marmots.
Now a new one does the rounds
Carried from gun to gun by varmints.

One leaves clear records of its genes
In teeth and bones,
From Smithfield to Italy.

The other spreads its memes
Through police who know no wrong
And internet publicity.

The present American horror show
May yet be remembered by a single poem.
People get tired of video.

I've seen this poem a dozen times
About just one guy who died.
Otherwise it's all the same.

Make no mistake that a news report,
Whatever that is in this day and age,
Whoever protests, whoever pays,

Lasts a single minute. Holinshed's lists
Of aristocrats who died for this and that
Come over slowly from Calais

On parchment strips, those will remain
While all things fade
From the digital consciousness.

Eric Garner. That was the name.
Let it be carried in the world mainframe
Until the canticle for Leibowitz.

Goodbye, Cecil, goodbye.
Alas, your radio collar smashed
And every talk show host unleashed

To cry on air, but not about those guys,
The hunter's guides in Zimbabwe
Who took the cash and now may die in jail.

Put the black men safely away.
They are not rare, with noble Aslan faces and straight hair.
In Minnesota one white man walks free

In the game park of midwestern liberty.
His dental practice is reviled.
Weep for Cecil. See Rhodesians smile.

66

What are we meant to feel at the raccoon funeral?
What is it that has died?
Rectitude or uptightness? Tact or pride?

Conrad the raccoon, like dozens of his mates
Was found dead this summer on a city street.
Garbage collectors, though this year not on strike,

Left him to grow ripe
For tweets and photo opps.
He trended Toronto-wide.

As usual that day, many people died,
The elderly, the premature, victims of assorted wars.
But Conrad the raccoon got the frills and furbelows.

Candles, red ribbons, roses, silver-framed photos
For his sidewalk shrine.

We are scared to death by the words for things.
Even yet, when we should know better.
I know my father's teeth will chatter

If I say *pneumonia* about my son.
Suddenly it is World War One
And influenza, H 1 N 1

And doom and liver flukes.
It's Bay of Pigs and waiting nukes.

And me? I am a heartless bitch
For saying he should get a grip.

68

I used to title everything.
But why say it twice?
A poem of thirty lines
Is not the Colosseum.

Vistas like those at Penshurst,
How often do we see them
Unfolding in the suburbs of our lives?
What if the reader wasn't primed?

What if I did not describe
The cold wind blowing across my lawn,
Wrinkling its arctic brow, the dropping crows
From the height of pines

And all the stark details that show
I'm a serious poet of the northern climes?
If under my Presbyterian gaze
The rusty nail, the swinging gate, the highway sky

Echoing and magnified
Just dried up and blew away?
Say something, anything, once. Say it direct.
Don't leave me palely to reflect

On the distance between your title's claim
And the minuscule evidences of things seen.
It's not the wilderness but the clear voice that cries
That we remember as we die.

69

Funeral strippers are a plague in China.
They're becoming enemies of the state
In an update of the *danse macabre*.

The dead repose in urns or coffins
While women shake asses and tassels
To accompany them to the jade mountain.

It has a throwback charm
But authorities worry about the tone.
Above all they worry lest

Children be exposed to the female breast.
The point is to ramp up the crowds
And feasts of food won't do it now.

They need more spectacle and more flesh.
The dead have honour to enhance
And so they sponsor dance that they don't even get to see,

Quite selflessly.
It's the new pomp and circumstance.
I see this as a great improvement

On the sanctimonious bowel movement
Of every funeral to which I've been
Or caught a glimpse of on TV.

Candle in the wind, indeed.
To mine I'll invite every stripper I know:
Give the grandkids a bit of a show.

I read an op ed in the *New York Times*
About an assisted suicide
In Belgium. The woman's beautiful Flemish name

Was Godelieva, which I adored.
She killed herself at age sixty-four
After a life of misery, therapy, pain and shame.

Intermittently she did quite well,
As the depressed and anxious can
But inevitably estranged

Everyone she touched, woman and man.
Madness eats all human trust.
We've always feared its contagiousness.

Godelieva's son kicked up a fuss
After her death. Guilt is the last duress
That the insane can exercise.

He complained that her doctor was a demagogue.
Perhaps he was. Yet he untied
A knot that bound five lives or more

With a single cut, after she had signed
And been assessed and filled out forms.
A bureaucratic death is fine

After a bureaucratic life. You still get to die
In all its primal force. That doesn't go away.
Only you do. You want to. You are tired

Or spiteful or want to be admired.
The plunger drops and it is moot.
But this way your death's the last thing you do.

And you, blessed, will never have to read
The dumbass comments on your meme.

The natives here once lost a genocidal war.
That's what happens when people come from afar
To take your land. It happens everywhere.

We took it. Bang. It's ours. Such is the fact.
No one has any intention of giving it back.
Nor could we, if it came to that.

Who cares if we apologize?
Such speech is wind. It will not rectify
The past and let them win.

And to deny it was a war insults us all.
War is still war, slow and colonial.
No one says wars are not equivocal

But some are clear, and every city planted here,
And every word and every law that guarantees all that you own
Tells us that ours was one of those.

Rilke was calm about death.
He thought the mind could stretch
Infinitely to compass it.

He thought it was our task
To eat the world and make it last
Inside us. Like bees, he said.

Jugful of honey, every head,
Containing experience's distillate.
Purer and sweeter than the first time round

Wherein the ever-evasive world is found.
Death splits our delicate sausage casing
And it oozes out, releasing

Itself into unseparateness.
And so, for Rilke, every death
Gilded and enriched the rest.

My son's imaginary friend just bit the dust:
Yukio the fabulous.

He was born on a Monday, fair of face.
The first day of our island stay.

He lived eleven days,
Protean, in rocks and waves.

At night he occupied stuffed toys.
Invisible, he biked beside.

He ran a magic portal between worlds:
This one and the digital.

Sometimes he was sand in a bottle.
A constant interlocutor.

He sickened when we went away,
Like any good *genius loci.*

He was weak and flushed.
My son told him not to get up.

He tucked him into his own bed.
Soon enough Yukio was dead.

Yukio!

The funeral is later today.
There will be dirges, bacon sandwiches, homemade punch
For Yukio, who was with us once.

In memoriam Tennyson said
Nine years of things about his friend
Who'd died. He brought him back by slow
Degrees, from sunsets, wind in the trees,

Gathering pieces painstakingly.
Tennyson, in his purity,
He never lied, never missed his line.
Grief became him metrically.

It made him blind. All he could see
Was Hallam's absence: the whole world
A cancelled cheque, crumpled and furled,
Unspent inside his pocketbook.

There its yellowing edges curled
Until his friend crept out, imbued
Everything and made it new.
At second look, he saw it through

Lost eyes, and it was dearer far
Than it had been before. A borrowed
Death does that for you. Your own cannot.
We each will miss the lesson that

We've taught. Compassion is what we learn
From those who die and don't return.
Grief gives us that hitch in the eye,
Catching on things as they pass by.

I don't read airport thrillers.
I don't watch movies about serial killers.
Nor have I ever cared for CSI.

Death's not a gambit I admire.
Not aphrodisiac or *apéritif.*
Beginning at the end is no relief.

Why twist and turn to unravel
The backward plots? See the judges bang their gavels?
Death always wins.

Meanings may be imposed, justice served or missed
And cases closed. So what?
The readers' and the writer's breath

Extend beyond the character's death.
We live. We learn. They only die. It's *schadenfreude* every time.
So much for the life of crime.

My kids would like to regenerate.
They don't want to die and we don't tolerate
Chat about God.

So they say, who would you like to be?
Patrick Troughton? I like the flute.
David Tennant's kind of cute.

Tom Baker's scarf makes me feel less scared.
And now there's Clara, who's everywhere.
And Captain Jack just keeps coming back, doesn't he?

It's a plague of immortality.

Social media infects my book of death
With its proud unflesh, its scars of emptiness.
The *bowge* of court grown huge, with lifeless breath
That makes all things its food: all bad, all good, unless
It is not cool. The home of formlessness, the end
Of sense, where numbers rule and everyone resents
Everyone in parallel. Where all of your friends
Complain of the police and are them yet.
Hyperbolic, hypermetric, phallocentric crap,
Where no small is too small and nothing's big enough.
Women who are raped stand up to be raped again,
Fostering our addiction to each other's pain.
The internet's the sickest thing the world has ever seen.
Vile to the core. After this one book, no more.

Please God this is the last sestina. Die.
It's brought to you by Stephen Fry. Please die.
By algorithm occluding rhyme. Die.
Auden shouting through his megaphone, die
Fascists! You unlearned, unwashed fools! Do die!
Or IVF for when our babies die

Or won't be born, the little swine. So, die
Ye gods of infertility! You die,
We live, the rich ones. Only the poor die
For lack of thee. Swinburne was right, a die-
Off's what we need: of shame and of blame, dy-
Adic sexuality. Die, squares, die!

Get them where they live, in poetry. Die
Then they will, assuredly. Straight lines die
And fall, crossed stanzas waterfall: just die
And end it all, confining rooms. To die
Is to rhyme, to fatally mark time. Die
And just spare us being twee. Let it die,

Let it go. Readers will never know. Die
On assonance-stretched rope. Last hope, go die.
Repetition is secure. The stupid (die!)
Know it's there, serial and pure. Die, die.
Self-similarity of sign. Art, die.
Artists, resign. Programmers rule. Thus die

The shaky tools of words. The king will die
And be made base two in the base court. Die
You shy, retiring fools. How then to die
Upon the sword you did not use? Fade, die
The shapes and bonds that words can make; they die
For modesty's sake. *Rum, ram, ruf:* they die

Bi lettre. God save us all from rap. Die,
All populist, flaky crap. What's left? Die
And see. Silence. Boring poetry. Die
In a host of magazines, where we die
In twelves. Our friends, our editors, who die
With our exhausted ghostly selves. Well, die

Then, if you must. Die, the journey; die,
The trust. Die, the craft. Just give it up and die.
Can't say I didn't ask. Can't think why. Die.

79

People do die of broken hearts.
My father-in-law has a torn
Aorta.

He's in the hospital
After years of feeling little worth.
His heart has long been out of sorts.

Our parts rebel
Against the things we put them through.
And so would you

If asked to beat and beat and beat
While other parts get to fuck and eat
As you're forever taking out the trash.

I guess it's the liver that does that.
The heart is the one-man bucket brigade:
Slop slop slop all day

Tucked away inside its cave of ribs,
Caliban to the Prospero brain.
Angry slave who kills us with its pain.

Here is a fresh peach pie.
Now, we have to tell you that your grandpa may die.
He's very sick. He's going into surgery.
There's nothing we can do. Just so you know.
You can cry, or not, about these things.
Just so you understand what happens when the phone rings.

While virtuous men pass mildly away
The rest of us die quite variously.
It can take a long time.

Processes are unclear.
Different kinds of tubes appear.
Teams of doctors come and go.

No one quite knows what's happening
As it seems that everything
Breaks down at once.

He's unresponsive. What? Well, why?
Here are five reasons he might die.
We're just not sure which ones obtain.

You're not? Well, not till he's awake.
Not till we do the scan.
And when is that? Ah, that would be when

He's strong enough to lie supine.
What? Flat? Look, right now, that's how he lies.
No, he does not. He's somewhat propped.

Otherwise his lungs fill up.
If things change, we'll let you know ASAP.
Yes, thanks. I understand.

Things are much less clear than you might think
Here at the brink.
It's very wide, though uniformly steep.

Geologic time used to be slow.
Unimaginably so.
Chthonically, things would unfold

In spans ten million years or more,
Measured in the lives of stones and river beds
And when volcanoes raised their hoary heads to blow.

Agriculture birthed ten thousand years ago.
We shaved the planet to expose its chops
And gave it enemas to boost the crops.

The Holocene. The globe was changed. The pace
Increased. We burrowed deep for coal and burned
The oily marrow of the planet's bones.

Released carbon heated up our air.
Now trapped beneath
The ozone layer, we boil away against the cold abyss.

The nimble Anthropocene:
Brief and bright, not ponderous and vast.
Fireflies flaming behind glass.

The preachers of doom
Have redesigned the natural history rooms
At the Museum.

Just walking through
Is now enough to make you paranoid.
It's not the blind glass eyes

Of still beasts from far and wide,
The bulbous fish immobilized,
But the small bleak signs

About the loss of biodiversity,
The somber mood that supersedes
The cabinet of curiosity.

True, it was always odd
To pin a wonder to a board.
But we walk through an elegy.

We just get over original sin, now this:
Our children forced to take the blame.
Debating, debating again and again:

Which is worth more –
This dwindling remnant here
Or all the stuff on all the other floors?

Art? Armour? Domestic furnishings?
Roman gold? The pyramids? The tale of steam
And coal and oil? Exploration? Human toil?

Textiles, inscriptions, deep-buried gems from bloody mines?
When I came to the Museum as a child
Choices were less stark.

I'd pat the stuffed raccoon, and then
Rush to the Madonnas and the Chinese art;
Burn past the dinosaurs, those empty bones,

To find clay pots and ornate shoes, the stolen truths
Of human lives: see what they ate and owned.
Who they killed with their mighty swords;

Who's buried in what tombs.
Then back to the natural history floor
To creep through the bat cave's eerie door,

Where I would dash through the sonorous drips
Just to prove I was not a wimp.
Now the gloomy route of the bat cave's traffic

Is far less scary than the infographics
On all the slender, silent screens
That stand among the quiet remains.

A guillotine is a strange machine
To an anglophone.
French. Swift-slow.

Long in the set-up, many parts integral,
But then, quick effect. Precise, repeatable.
We just use rope.

Versatile. Stretchy.
And any old tree
Will do.

Apocalypse is a word that breeds
Because people don't know what it means.
A plague of robots, zombies, acronyms,
Well-fed distressed teens.
Creeping neoteny may get us in the end.
Apocalypse, the final youthful trend.

Revelation is the best translation, though.
Not the moment when it ends; the moment when you know.
William Langland, in 1381
Thought that the apocalypse lived in his London.
London, way back then.
Powerful, eager city, where people went to spend.

He saw lies and waste.
People spent their time doing the opposite
Of everything they claimed,
Constrained by money's power.
That was his final hour
And we have known since then.

86

Tennyson felt a mysterious spirit
Beyond the horizon, or in it, or near it,
Creeping across the crest of the world
A shadow of brightness, a meaning revealed.

He brought incarnation right the way home
And planted his friend in his sister's womb
On her wedding day. All the bells pealed.
Hallam rose from his tomb and his flesh was unsealed

Into sky, into hill, holt, field, wold, weald,
Into things, into words, and into the girl,
His exile repealed. Energy is not lost –
But somebody's got to be willing to host.

87

Sometimes you take your death into your own hands
And refuse to buy godawful pre-paid plans.

A family friend is using up the wood scraps in his shop
To build himself a coffin. It's good enough, he says.
He goes down to the basement and works on it on slow days.

The final DIY. I wonder if they'd open up a new Home
   Depot aisle.
Beautiful coffin beech. Interesting hinges. Material for wreaths
For the more soft-core. A range of urn glazes. Check out
   over here.

The world has always been hard to find.
We've thrown out the fruit and left the rind.
Faces glow through diaphanous screens

And tell us how it ought to be.
They speak in tongues, in light and shadow
And video games are played by adults.

The children are wearing their mother's shoes.
A few more years and they'll rule the roost
As the boomers finally learn to die,

At last outrun by their technology.
Machines in their silent factories
Have won.

They're not our servants but our friends
As Rilke said, in 1910.

Tonight the fattened mermaids sing
To issue in the internet of things.
Let me tell you what you can do with that misnomer.
I sit here gloomily and think of Homer,

On the dimming beach, as drifts of trash
Clatter softly against my ankles,
The melancholy, long, withdrawing roar
Of everything a humanist holds dear.

Skyward the sad elite have all withdrawn,
To their electric world. They've pulled it on
Over the old like a transparent plastic glove.

I hear them pinging dismally afar.
Here on the quiet earth that I still love,
Where the last humans are.

ACKNOWLEDGMENTS

An earlier version of poem number 39 appeared in *The New Quarterly* 136 (Fall 2015).

Thanks to Jeffery Donaldson and Danila Sokolov for commenting on early drafts. My gratitude also to the staff and designers at MQUP, especially to Ryan Van Huijstee who caught a science blooper at the last minute.